MAKE 'EM LAUGH
(Sitcom Length)

Jason Odell Williams

LICENSING & PRODUCTION INQUIRIES
Uproar Theatrics, LLC.
hello@uproartheatrics.com | www.UproarTheatrics.com

<u>CAST</u>: (7 - 21 performers, any age or gender)
The play can be cast with anywhere from 7 - 21 performers.
How roles are doubled, tripled or even quadrupled is left to
the creative team. (For instance, Gran and Norman can be
played by the same person! And it gives the play an extra
layer of meaning.) The ages, genders and races of the
performers don't matter. They can be high school students, or
college students, or in their 40s, or senior citizens, or
anything in between with any combination of all of the
above. There even are opportunities for cameos and surprise
casting. If the cast size is in the smaller range which means
there is a lot of doubling and tripling, don't worry about
trying to fool the audience or make the characters changes
backstage. Character/costume changes can happen in full
view of the audience and be done with a simple wig, prop,
costume piece and the accent/attitude of the new character.
Have fun with it!

<u>SETTING</u>:
A living room set that resembles a popular American sitcom.
There is a sofa roughly centerstage, a kitchen table and
kitchen area UR, a balcony offstage, and 4 doorframes (front
door SR, a bedroom door DSL, a second bedroom door USL,
and a bathroom door US Middle/Right). There do not have
to be WALLS. The set should look real _and_ surreal at the
same time. As if an amalgam of lots of popular sitcom sets
but also a dream so not everything is normal.

<u>TONE/INSPIRATION</u>:
The tone of this play for the most part is that of the classic
multi-cam sitcom. Timing is everything. For the main
section of the play, shows to watch for inspiration would be
Friends, Will & Grace, and *The Golden Girls.* For the one-
liners (and just because they are also great shows!) you can
also check out *Alice, Diff'rent Strokes, Good Times, Family
Matters*, *Happy Days, Mork & Mindy, The Big Bang Theory,
Get Smart,* and *The Mary Tyler Moore Show.*

SOUND EFFECTS (SFX):

Various sound effects (SFX) are used throughout the play, notably "laughs" from a sitcom laugh track: small, medium and big. Also, Ooooo's and Ahhh's from a studio audience. Basically anything you might hear from the studio audience during a multi-camera sitcom broadcast.

NOTES ON TEXT:

- A slash ("// ") denotes a point of overlap between one speaker's line and the next speaker's line.
- Text in brackets [...] indicate a thought expressed non-verbally.

NOTES ON LANGUAGE:

A digital "TV-G" version of this script is available upon request. Please email licenses@uproartheatrics.com to learn more, or visit UproarTheatrics.com

CHARACTERS:

PRESENT DAY
GRAN
KID
PROMPT 1
PROMPT 2
PROMPT 3
SHADOWY FIGURE / NORMAN LEAR

1990'S SITCOM ABOUT SIX FRIENDS LIVING IN NEW YORK CITY
JIMMY
MELISSA
FRANKIE

1990'S SITCOM ABOUT A WOMAN WITH A GAY ROOMMATE IN NYC
CHASE
JACQUES
KATHLEEN

1980'S SITCOM ABOUT FOUR OLDER WOMEN LIVING TOGETHER IN FLORIDA
BLAIR
RUTH
SYLVIA

CATCHPHRASE MASH-UPS FROM CLASSIC SITCOMS
CATCHPHRASE 1
CATCHPHRASE 2
CATCHPHRASE 3
CATCHPHRASE 4
CATCHPHRASE 5
CATCHPHRASE 6

SCENE 1

*Lights up on GRAN & KID sitting on a sofa in a
darkened living room. An unseen TV plays in
front of them. Gran watches TV while Kid types
on a laptop.*

SFX: A big LAUGH from a laugh track on TV.

Gran laughs then looks over at Kid.

GRAN

What's 'a matter, Kid? You forget how to laugh?

KID

I'd laugh if something was funny. ... Also, kinda busy here?
(nods at the laptop)

GRAN

Whattya doin' - postin' Tick Tacks or something?

KID
(smiles at Gran's gaff)
Bookkeeping for Mom & Dad's store.

GRAN

Tsh. This is what's wrong with your generation. Too serious
all the time.

KID

Well, there's a lot to be serious about. In addition to my job
after school, there's climate change, gun violence, abortion
rights, LBGTQ rights, not to mention the mental health crisis
that social media // is causing--

GRAN

Which is why you should take a break and laugh with your old Gran. I know life can seem tough, but everyone thinks *their* generation has it the worst. I had Vietnam. My *parents* had the Great Depression.

KID

What about my mom and dad? What crisis did they live through?

GRAN

I don't know... Grunge music? The point is - everyone has crosses to bear. So stopping to laugh once in a while is never a bad idea.

KID

No time to stop. Gotta think about the future. And for me that's getting through high school then going right to work full-time at Mom & Dad's store.

GRAN

The store? No, Kid - you're better than that! Didn't you wanna to go to college and study to be the next great TV writer? Wasn't that your dream since you could talk?

KID

Pipe dreams, Gran. The smart move is to save the tuition and student loan money and go straight into the workforce.

GRAN

Are you saying there isn't even a small part of you that wants to be a writer anymore?

KID

It's not practical. And even if it was, I'd never write stuff like that. *(gestures at TV)* How can you watch this junk over and over?

GRAN
(wistful)

Junk? These are the best sitcoms ever produced. All classics!

KID

Comedy is dead! The only thing people watch now are superhero movies and moody dramas on Netflix.

GRAN

Tsh. Whatever happened to Dick Van Dyke and Mary Tyler Moore!

KID

Are those friends of yours?

GRAN

Seriously? What are they teaching you in that school?

KID

How to take the A.C.T.

GRAN

Is that a pill for anxiety?

KID

No. But it doesn't matter cuz I'm not going to college anyway.

GRAN

You should at least _apply_. In case you DO wanna write some day, or do anything other than work at that boring store... you're gonna need a college education. I mean, have you even looked at the applications? They're due pretty soon, right?

KID

Next week, I think?

GRAN

Then what are you doing fartin' around watching TV? Get crackin'!

Gran turns off the TV with the remote.

KID

I wasn't even watching that! And didn't you _just_ tell me that stopping to laugh is never a bad idea??

GRAN

You're listening to _me_ now?!!?

KID

But what's the point of college? Anything I _don't_ learn in high school, I can learn from YouTube.

GRAN

You can't learn how to _write_ from YouTube! _Or_ Chat GPT!

KID

I told you, I don't wanna be a writer anymore!

GRAN

Listen, Kid. I love ya. But your mom and dad always said education was their number one priority for ya, and I gotta respect their wishes... *(sighs, puts a comforting hand on the Kid's shoulder)* now that they're gone.

KID

They're not dead - they're at a conference for small business owners.

While talking, Gran stands behind the couch and swaps the real TV remote with a "magic remote" that is a different shape/color.

GRAN

Still. That means I'm in charge this week. And I say: Apply to college, see what happens! And if you get stuck...

She hands him the "magic remote."

GRAN

Try watching some of those classic sitcoms. Relax your mind... let divine inspiration flow... and before ya know it... you might just find... *Your True Passion*.

She winks and exits.

The Kid looks at the remote. Huh. Different. Shrugs, whatever. Sets the remote aside, grabs the laptop and opens it.

KID

All right, lemme bang out this application to make Gran happy. Shouldn't be too hard. What were those essay prompts again...?

The Kid taps a few keys.

A spotlight up on PROMPT #1

PROMPT 1
Common application, essay prompt number one: Discuss an accomplishment or event that marked your transition from childhood to adulthood within your culture, community, or family.

KID
Has that even happened to me yet?

A spotlight up on PROMPT #2

PROMPT 2
Common app, essay prompt number two: Recount an incident or time when you experienced failure. How did it affect you, and what lessons did you learn?

KID
Experienced failure? How about like -- *all the time?*

A spotlight up on PROMPT #3

PROMPT 3
Essay prompt number three: Reflect on a time when you challenged a belief or idea. What propelled you to act? Would you make the same decision again?

PROMPT 1
Oh yeah. I like that one.

PROMPT 2
Yes! *SO* much better than mine.

KID

....Guys. Please? I'm trying to think here.

PROMPT 1

Right, of course. Our bad.

PROMPT 2

Sorry, yes. You do you.

KID

Jeez, I just--- Nothing cool has ever happened to me. This is why I didn't want to do this - I can't write an essay about my life when I have no idea what I want to *do* with my life!! This is totally pointless!

> *The Kid puts the laptop aside (still open) and sits back. The Prompts step into the shadows but don't exit.*

KID

Maybe I need a break. Like Gran said. Relax my mind... And divine inspiration will flow.

> *The Kid grabs the magic remote. Presses the power button, but nothing happens.*
>
> *Kids shakes the remote. Presses the power button again. Still nothing.*
>
> *The Kid then presses a few different buttons and this time, the LIGHTS flicker and go funky.*

KID
(looking around)

...Did I do that?

A SHADOWY FIGURE wearing a poplin fabric sport hat enters in backlight (maybe a fog machine effect too??!) and tugs their own earlobe (ala Carol Burnett.)

KID

Whoa - who's that? What's going on? Why are you tugging your earlobes?! WHAT'S HAPPENING???

*The Prompts tug their earlobes in response to the Shadowy Figure... and the Kid suddenly **lays back, asleep / hypnotized.***

The Shadowy Figure nods to the Prompts. "It's on." Then the Shadowy Figure exits.

All of the Prompts then do the "Wayne's World" flashback move, wiggling their arms in front of their faces as they say:

THE 3 PROMPTS
(wiggling arms in front of faces)

Doo-doo-loo-doo. Doo-doo-loo-doo. Doo-doo-loo-doo. Doo-doo-loo-doo.

The lights go OUT.

SCENE 2

Lights up full and bright. It's happy sitcom lighting. The entire set is revealed. It looks a LOT like the set of the sitcom Friends.

The Kid is still asleep on the couch, laptop on belly.

MELISSA enters.

SFX: Studio audience APPLAUSE, plus hoots and cheers.

She wears rubber cleaning gloves and carries a sponge and rag in her hands. She begins wiping down a countertop (or table, or wall) going over and over a spot with fervor.

MELISSA
Out, damned spot! out, I say!

SFX: Small LAUGH from the studio audience.

Then the front door opens. It's JIMMY.

SFX: Studio audience APPLAUDS even louder with even more WHOOPS.

JIMMY
Hey.

MELISSA
(not looking up from her cleaning)

Hey.

JIMMY

Where's your brother? He's supposed to drive me to Jersey
this afternoon.

MELISSA

What's in Jersey?

JIMMY

You kidding? What's NOT in Jersey? You got the shore. You
got the Boss! And most of all.... You got _sandwiches_.

SFX: BIG LAUGH into APPLAUSE.

*The Kid darts awake! [NOTE: the "magic
remote" should be somewhere on the couch.]*

KID

What's happening where am I -- WHOA!! WHO ARE YOU
PEOPLE?!

JIMMY

Hey, Charlie.

MELISSA

Hey, sleepy head.

*She goes to the Kid, holding her rubber-gloved
hands up like a surgeon and quickly kisses the
Kid hello. (Can be on the cheek, on the head, or
she can blow him a kiss from across the room).*

MELISSA

Mwah!

SFX: Studio audience, OOOOOO!

KID

Uh... what?

MELISSA

I said, hey sleepy head.

> *She goes to kiss the Kid again but the Kid stands quickly and backs away.*

KID

Nuh-nuh-nuh.... I heard you. I just--- wh-- wh. Wait. You're... you're Melissa.

MELISSA

Uh. Yeah?

KID

And you're Jimmy!

JIMMY

Last time I checked.

KID

Whoa! I, I, I, I mean... don't ever tell my Gran, but... I love you guys!

MELISSA	JIMMY
Awww. We love you!	Back atcha buddy.

KID

But I don't understand how I'm -- what exactly is happening here?

Melissa goes back to cleaning.

JIMMY

What's happening is, it's Saturday. So we're going to Jersey for some serious sandwiches and not-so-serious minor league baseball.

Jimmy makes a "crack of the bat" sound while swinging an imaginary baseball ball bat and then makes his own fake crowd cheer sound.

SFX: Medium laugh.

KID

Wait. Did you hear that?

JIMMY
(proud)

My fake crowd noise? Sounds like you're *at* the stadium, right?

SFX: Medium laugh.

KID
(pointing up and around him at the sound)

No -- *that!* The laughing! The clapping. The ooh'ing and ahh'ing when she kissed me!

MELISSA

Aw! You hear ooh's and ahh's when we kiss? I hear the theme song from Titanic.

JIMMY

Don't a bunch of people die at the end of that movie?

MELISSA

I don't know. I always turn it off before they hit the iceberg.

SFX: Medium laugh.

KID

.... WHAT ARE YOU PEOPLE TALKING ABOUT?!!?!

JIMMY   MELISSA

Titanic.   Titanic.

KID

Okay. This is just a dream. I can wake up. Ready... WAKE UP!

Nothing happens.

KID

NOW! .... And NOW!

Nothing.

KID
(checking pockets for phone)
Whatever. I'll just order a car. What's the address here?

MELISSA

Charlie! You know the address! You've lived in New York your entire life.

KID

I'm in New York...? CITY?!?! *(gives up checking pockets because they found nothi*ng.) And great! I don't even have my phone!... Oh, oh! I know. *(to Jimmy)* Hit me.

JIMMY

What?

KID

Hit me, slap me, pinch me! I need to jolt my system in the dream so I'll wake up for real.

JIMMY

No idea what you're talking about - but I like hitting people, so here goes.

Jimmy smacks Kid. Slow burn.

KID

...Ow!

JIMMY

You're welcome.

SFX: Medium laugh.

Kid looks around.

KID

No. No! I'm still here. You're still here. Why are we still here? What kind of sick twisted nightmare is this? Trapped inside a sitcom after trying to apply to college -- WHICH I WAS ONLY DOING 'CAUSE GRAN *BEGGED* ME TO! AND NOW I HAVE *NO* IDEA HOW TO GET OUT OF HERE, LET ALONE WHAT I'M GONNA DO WITH THE REST OF MY LIFE!!

*Kid suddenly flings the laptop on the ground,
then completely regrets it a second later and
makes a wincing face, like, "Oh no, did I just
break my laptop?!"*

SFX: Studio audience, "Oooooo."

MELISSA
...Looks like someone woke up on the wrong side of the
couch.

SFX: Big laugh and applause.

Guitar music sting.

AD BREAK

*Prompt 1 enters and talks directly to the
audience.*

PROMPT 1
If you're like me, you're busy and need a break from it all.
What with school, sports, play rehearsal, volunteering, not to
mention finding time to hang with your... FRIENDS.

*Prompts 2 & 3enter. Prompt 2 holds a SKIP AD
sign. They watch Prompt 1 for a beat.*

PROMPT 1
So when life gets busy, I like to relax with a warm, calming
cup of--

*Prompt 3 presses the SKIP AD sign multiple
times. Lights shift and Prompt 1 changes their*

demeanor and now talks like a weightlifting bro.

PROMPT 1
(weightlifting bro)
DO YOU EVEN LIFT, BRO? OF COURSE YOU DO!
THAT'S WHY YOU NEED THE NEWEST PROTEIN
SUPPLEMENT FROM THE MAKERS OF "MEGA-X-
BRO-BUILD" AND "SHREDDER-EXTREME"
CALLED...

PROMPT 2 & PROMPT 3
"TRIPLE X-RADICAL-BRO-BUILD-SHRED!!"

PROMPT 1
Just listen to these testimonials from actual Bro-Build users.

PROMPT 2
(weightlifting bro)
I lift. Drink Bro-build. Lift more. Shred more. And feel
totally jacked!

PROMPT 3
Me, too! I also have trouble going to the bathroom. But who
cares when you have abs like this? (*Lifts shirt to show off
abs. The abs can be naturally great, naturally NOT great, or
clearly fake washboard abs.*) Thanks, Triple-X-Radical-Bro-
Build-Shred!"

PROMPT 1
To order yours - click on the link below.

PROMPT 2 & PROMPT 3
AND GET SHREDDED NOW!

(talks super fast)

The makers of Bro-build are not responsible for any side effects which can include night blindness, day blindness, forgetting your name, and turning into a total moron. Offer not valid in Canada or Mexico.

The Prompts high five then exit. Lights shift.

SCENE 3

Tight spot up on just Kid asleep on the couch.

Kid wakes with a jolt. Looks around. Alone.

KID

Oh good! Okay... It was just a dream. I'm home and everything is back to nor--

Lights up full as CHASE enters wearing a robe.

CHASE

Bill! Where have you been?

SFX: Audience cheers! Chase "holds" like a pro during the applause.

CHASE

You _know_ I have a really important date tonight! ...So naturally I'd rather be _complaining_ about it to you.

SFX: Medium laugh. Kid looks around confused.

                            KID
Uh... sorry?

                           CHASE
Never mind. Come here...

          She pulls Kid further into the room.

                           CHASE
I need the opinion of a smart, stylish, successful gay man....
But you'll do in a pinch.

          SFX: Medium laugh.

          *Then Chase dramatically drops her robe to
          reveal she's wearing an elegant dress
          underneath. The audience WHOOO's.*

                           CHASE
I'm going for Julia Roberts but I'll settle for Julia Louis-
Dreyfus. *(Pause)* Oh who am I kidding, I'd settle for Julia
Child.

          SFX: BIG laugh.

          *Kid looks around again, confused, when the
          door FLIES open and...*

          *JACQUES enters (Male, flamboyant,
          pronounces his name "Sz-ahk" - the French
          way). He darts across the stage to the
          refrigerator and gets a bottle of water as he
          says...*

18

JACQUES

Oh my gosh, you guys. *(pointing to Kid)* And gals. But I just
had the best audition ever! They called me in for Chorus Boy
#7 and I said, "Hey! Jacques don't take parts with a number
no mo'," and they told me to get lost, rightly so -- has your
fridge always been over here? - it's weird and I LOVE IT!
(grabs bottle of water, continues) - but on the elevator ride
down *leaving* the audition I bumped into this *other* casting
director who said they were looking for actors-slash-dancers-
slash-high energy personalities-slash-vegan-life-coaches and
I said, O.M.G. that's me to a T.T.T. So she handed me some
pages, dragged my butt off the elevator on the 4th floor, had
me cold read with the director and sham-a-lamma-ding-
dong, they hired me on the spot!

> *The audience LAUGHS & CHEERS while
> Jacques takes a long swig of water, catching his
> breath.*

CHASE

Jacques, that's amazing! What's the part?

JACQUES

Waiter #3.

> *SFX: Big laugh.*

JACQUES

But he has a checkered past, a real backstory, ya know.

> *Chase nods seriously. Kid is still in shock. He's
> about to say something when...*

> *KATHLEEN enters through the still open front
> door. (Female, rich, confident, speaks with a
> high voice.) She's holding a half-full martini.*

KATHLEEN

There you are, Jacques-y-poo. Driver and I have been
looking all over - ya left your dang fanny pack in my limo -
and the only fanny's I want in my limo are _actual_ fannies!

JACQUES

Kathleen, I'm so sorry, but my head's just all over the place
now that I've been cast as a featured-extra on a NETWORK
SITCOM!

SFX: The audience cheers.

KATHLEEN

Oh, Jacques-y boy, puddin' 'n' pie! You didn't tell me you
got the gosh-darn part!

JACQUES

Ooo, I was just telling Bill and Chase - see, what had
happened was--

KID

I'm sorry, can we take a time out, please!!??

JACQUES	KATHLEEN
Shut up, Bill.	Shut up, Bill.

> _Jacques and Kathleen look at each other and_
> _bust out laughing for both having said the same_
> _thing at the same time. Chase watches amused_
> _but a little embarrassed/sad for Kid/Bill._

KATHLEEN

(can hardly catch her breath, she's laughing so hard)
O-M-G... We both... told Bill... to shut up... at the same
time!!

JACQUES
(can hardly catch his breath, he's laughing so hard)
It's true... Bill... is so... stupid!

Jacques and Kathleen laugh harder. Chase goes to Kid.

CHASE
Bill - Bill. Forget these *Meshuggeneh,* I'm in a real pickle, and it's not about my date or this outfit. I need help from my favorite *Mench.* Cuz you're *Mishpucha* to me. So listen: I feel like the clock is ticking -- my biological one -- and I don't mean to *Kvetch* like a *Putz,* but *Oy Vey,* if you'd finally consider doing IVF with me it'd be a real *Shanda,* ya know what I'm saying?

KID
I have no _idea_ what you're saying. Was any of that English?

Kathleen pulls Kid away from Chase for a more "private chat."

KATHLEEN
Can I borrow him for a sec - thanks. So Bill, I don't know what that floozy's been sayin' about me, but ain't true I tells ya! That car was already totaled when I got there, and now the police are dropping by my house asking questions-- and I mean the _real_ police, not the fun kind who wear short-shorts and disco dance to Donna Summer. It's freakin' me out and I feel like I'm gonna *Plotz! Oy Vey!* I'm startin' to talk like Chase! *(shakes Kid by the shoulders)* What do I do, Bill, what do I do?!

Before Kid can reply, Jacques comes over and pulls Kid away for a more private chat.

JACQUES

Mmm, canIborrowhimforasec - thanks. Hey pal, so I don't
know what these two have been saying or why they're
asking for private advice, but you know how I hate feeling
left out, so I'm just gonna talk for a few seconds while you
nod and act like I'm saying something smart and classy that
needs your immediate attention, *(shakes Kid by the
shoulders)* 'cause I don't wanna be the only one not getting
advice!!!

CHASE

Okay, okay - let's give Bill some room. Sheesh....

Chase pulls Kid aside.

CHASE

Hey. Seriously. What's the matter, Bill? You seem different.

KID

That's because I *am* different. I'm not your-gay-roommate-
slash-one-time-love-interest-now-co-dependant best friend.
I'm just a kid. Trying to find my way home and figure out
my life.

CHASE

...That may be the most honest thing you've ever said.

KID

Because it's true!

CHASE

I know it *feels* like it's true. Everyone suffers from imposter
syndrome. But that just means you're on the right path.

KID

No, it means I'm an actual imposter. Look. Touch my hair,
my arms, my face

*Chase touches Kid's arms and hair and is
starting to see maybe this isn't Bill....*

KID

I mean, do I even look old enough to have a kid with you
through IVF?!

*Jacques and Kathleen do perfectly timed SPIT
TAKES (straight out).*

JACQUES

Holy Moses supposes his toeses are roses!!

KATHLEEN

Bill and Chase are gonna have a _baby_ together?!

JACQUES

That means we'll be the gosh-darn Godparents and get to
shower them with gifts, by which I mean _you'll_ pay for
everything and I'll sign my name to the card.

*Kathleen and Jacques jump up and down super
excited, giggling, then do the "touch bellies"
move as they shout...*

JACQUES

Mazel Tov!

KATHLEEN

Mazel Tov!

KATHLEEN

Let's get Driver to take us to Neiman Marcus right now.

JACQUES

Does Neiman Marcus have stuff for babies?

KATHLEEN

Who cares -- mama needs a new pair of shoes!

Jacques and Kathleen exit. Chase looks at her watch (or a clock nearby).

CHASE

Oo! I gotta go, too - my date's in five minutes! We'll talk about the baby thing later okay - but Jacques and Kathleen seem happy. Mwah! Love you, Bill.

Chase exits.

KID

(really annoyed)

FOR THE LAST TIME, I'M NOT BILL! WHAT'S HAPPENING RIGHT NOW?

Lights shift.

SCENE 4

NORMAN LEAR enters. (From the audience, or a hidden entrance, but not from the front door of the apartment.) [PS. Norman was the Shadowy Figure from earlier!]

NORMAN LEAR

"What's Happening!" Great show, Kid. Not one of mine, but a terrific show.

KID

Whoa. Who are you?

NORMAN LEAR

Don't you recognize me by my signature hat? I'm legendary writer-producer and godfather of the modern sitcom... Norman Lear.

KID

...Cool?

NORMAN LEAR

Lemme guess. You never heard of me.

KID

Don't take it personally??

NORMAN LEAR

And you wanna be a TV writer?

KID

That was something I said out loud once -- when I was ten. Does that mean it has to be my life's ambition?

NORMAN LEAR

No, of course not. But this glimpse you're getting now? The magical reality device that only happens in movies, television and theatre? Regular people don't get this kind of glimpse. Only a special few. Which means you must be special. And exactly where you're supposed to be. Almost.

KID

Almost what? Almost outta here, almost home? I got no idea
what you're talking about!

NORMAN LEAR

Okay. You ever seen *A Christmas Carol?*

KID

No.

NORMAN LEAR

It's a Wonderful Life?

KID

Maybe parts of it on TV?

NORMAN LEAR

The Wizard of Oz?!

KID

Psh. Everyone's seen *The Wizard of Oz.*

NORMAN LEAR

I wasn't so sure with you, Kid. But in that movie, you know
how Dorothy gets bonked on the head then travels to Oz, has
a bunch of adventures, then suddenly wakes up and it was all
a dream but she's a changed person?

KID

Yeah...?

NORMAN LEAR

That's a glimpse! A look into your subconscious to uncover
your deepest fears, your wildest aspirations, your hopes and
dreams for the future. A chance to unlock your true passion.
Pretty great, huh?

                              KID
Uh, no! Dorothy got to sing and dance with the Tin Man and
the Scarecrow, I've been bouncing between sitcom sets
while getting yelled at and spit on by everyone!

                        NORMAN LEAR
Figuring out your passion can be difficult -- and painful --
and sloppy. But it's worth it.

                              KID
Okay - so how do I figure out what my passion is and get out
of here?

                        NORMAN LEAR
Gotta figure that out for yourself, Kid. Good luck!

            Norman tips his hat and exits.

                              KID
Seriously...?! Wow. Thanks for nuthin', old man. Sheesh.

            The Kid looks around.

                              KID
What am I supposed to do now?

                *Lights shift as Prompt 1 pops a head through a
                curtain or from behind a door.*

                          PROMPT 1
Psst. Hey, Kid. Over here!

                              KID
Are you talking to me? I thought you were just the YouTube
ads I had to skip through to--

Prompts 2 & 3 poke their heads into view.

PROMPT 2
(to Prompt 1)
We don't have much time! Just tell the kid what they need to hear.

KID
What are you all talking about?

PROMPT 3
The powers-that-be HATE when the ads stop "selling" and "get real" with people.

KID
Why?

PROMPT 2
It's super complicated and we don't have time to get into it, just trust us. It's bad.

PROMPT 3
Real bad.

KID
So what do you need to tell me?

> *The Prompts look around to make sure no one is listening...*

PROMPT 1
The only way to get a different result... is to try something new.

KID

...okay...?

PROMPT 2

Remember how you got here...?

KID

Yeah?

PROMPT 3

Maybe you need to press some different buttons...? See if
they take you somewhere... different?

KID

You mean back home?

> *The Prompts look at each other. Then back at the
> Kid.*

PROMPT 1

Sure, let's go with that.

PROMPT 2

Good luck, Kid!

> *The Prompts high five as they run off.*
>
> *Kid looks at the remote confused.*

KID

Welp. Here goes nothing.

> *The Kid presses a few other buttons. The lights
> shift. The Kid looks hopeful as...*

SCENE 5

RUTH, BLAIR and SYLVIA enter. (They should look like old ladies from the 1980s, and Sylvia is the oldest-looking.) Kid watches and listens intently, hoping they'll provide a clue about how to get home.

BLAIR
(she has a Southern accent)
Ruth, I don't understand why you won't go to the concert with me.

RUTH
Well, you know how back home in St. Elsa, North Dakota, I was voted the girl in high school most likely to get stuck in a trombone?

Blair sort of nods.

RUTH
Ever since then, I've stayed as far away from live music as possible.

SFX: Medium laugh.

BLAIR
Did you ever get stuck in a trombone?

RUTH
No, because I stay away from them!

SFX: Big laugh.

SYLVIA

Tell me, Ruth, did it hurt when they dropped you on your head so many times as a baby?

RUTH

Oh heavens, no. Doctors always told me I have a very thick skull.

SFX: Medium laugh.

BLAIR

Ruth, honey, I think sometimes you might want to keep those little anecdotes to yourself.

RUTH

But it's nothing to be ashamed of. My Mee-Maw used to say, "A thick skull just means..." Oh jeez, I can't remember what she used to say. Probably from being dropped on my head so much as a baby.

SYLVIA

I liked it better when she was talking about trombones.

SFX: Medium laugh.

RUTH

Speaking of trombones, back in St. Elsa, North Dakota, we had a cow named "Big Tuba."

BLAIR

I know I'm gonna regret this, but... why was your cow named "Big Tuba?"

RUTH

Because when she passed gas, it sounded like a big tuba! *(makes a tuba-like sound)*

SFX: Big laugh.

SYLVIA
"Big Tuba!" Sounds like Blair after she eats too much cheese!

BLAIR
Sylvia, I'll have you know that I've decided to take the high road when it comes to your petty jokes about my perceived flatulence-problem.

SYLVIA
What's to "perceive"? We share a wall - I _hear_ it every night.

SFX: Big laugh.

BLAIR
Dotty, will you please tell your elderly yet immature mother that I am taking the high road?!

Pause.

BLAIR
Dotty!

KID
Oh, me? Am I Dotty?

SYLVIA
And I thought Ruth was the simple one.

SFX: Medium laugh.

RUTH
Thank you, Sylvia!

SYLVIA

It wasn't a compliment.

SFX: Medium laugh. Ruth looks confused then shrugs it off.

BLAIR

Dotty! Are you going to defend my honor or not?!

SYLVIA

Blair, the last person to defend your honor fought in the war. The Civil War.

SFX: Medium laugh.

BLAIR

Dotty - will you please help!?

KID
(to themself)

Right. Maybe I need to learn some kind of lesson before moving forward: Defend people's honor and whatnot. *(clears throat,, then says to Sylvia)* Okay, uh... "Ma?" I think you should... leave Blair alone?

SYLVIA

And I think Menopause should happen to *men*, but life ain't perfect.

SFX: Medium laugh.

RUTH

Back in St. Elsa, North Dakota, we had an 80 year old woman who *never* went through menopause. She got pregnant at 82.

BLAIR

How is that possible?

RUTH

Her boyfriend was 37.

SFX: Big laugh.

SYLVIA
(stands up)
Ladies. I just had a sudden urge to go to St. Elsa, North
Dakota - who's with me?

> *Blair and Ruth both raise their hands, for
> different reasons.*

RUTH

Really, girls? Oh you'll love it. And if we leave now, we can
make it in time for the Cheese Parade.

SYLVIA

No cheese for Blair. Makes her toot like a tuba!

> *SFX: Big laugh as Ruth, Blair and Sylvia exit.*

KID

Wait, you can't leave - I haven't figured out how to get outta
here!

> *But they are already gone.*

KID

Wait a minute...

> *Kid looks at the remote. Presses a couple of*

different buttons. Nothing happens.

*Kid gets frustrated and presses every button on
the remote at once. The lights go wacky as...*

SCENE 6

*The room is suddenly flooded with new actors
(or the other actors quickly changing
personalities and adding wardrobe touches to
reflect a new character) as everyone shouts
mash-ups of famous sitcom catchphrases.*

CATCHPHRASE 1
Kiss my grits! -- Whatchoo talkin' bout?

CATCHPHRASE 2
To the moon, Bazinga! To the moon!

CATCHPHRASE 3
How YOU doin'? DynoMITE!

CATCHPHRASE 4
Yada yada yada - no soup for you!

CATCHPHRASE 5
Na-nu-na-nu. Missed it by THAT much!

CATCHPHRASE 6
(giving a thumbs' up like Fonzie)
Ayyyyyye! *(like Steve Urkel)* Did I do that?

THE 3 PROMPTS
(singing)
You're gonna make it after all! Dah-dah-DAH-dahhh-dun!

As they sing (now wearing berets) they spin around and throw the berets in the air.

KID

STOOOOOOOPPPPPP!!!

Everyone and everything freezes while the Kid continues.

KID

I need everyone to stop! Please. I don't want this, this, this...
GLIMPSE anymore! It's not helping me figure out anything!
So can you all just like... go away? Can I turn the channel or
unplug the Wi-Fi or... how do I get rid of you?

Everyone on stage slowly unfreezes and looks at the Kid.

KID

I don't mean to be a downer. I know you all thought I was
your Charlie or... Bill or Dotty! But I'm not. I'm just a kid
from nowhere who has no idea what I want to do with my
life. When I was younger, I wanted to be a comedy writer.
But there's so much content now it all blends together into
one big mash-up and we can't even remember what we
watched yesterday -- so what's the point of *any* of it?

Everyone sort of shrugs, mumbling and ad libbing as they go. ["Yeah, the kid makes a good point." "Guess we should get outta here." "I'm kinda hungry anyway." "Who wants pizza?!"]

*But no one leaves through the practical doors.
They exit into the audience, or into the wings
around flats, or through passageways we've
never seen anyone use before. It should feel
disorienting and 4th-wall breaking, like
watching a rehearsal end.*

SCENE 7

*The only ones left on stage are the actors
playing the Kid, Melissa, Jimmy and a new
character, FRANKIE, who has a GUITAR.*

FRANKIE

Wait! Do you really think there's no point to this?

KID

I'm sorry - who are you?

FRANKIE

Duh. I'm Frankie. Melissa's dopey but adorable friend who
plays ironic songs in the coffee shop about stinky cats and
the meaning of life.

KID

And you've been here this whole time?

FRANKIE

I think so...? Anyway, if you think this is pointless -- then our
entire existence is also pointless -- and that can't be true!

KID

Look, if TV's taught me anything it's that there's always a
larger life lesson to be learned at the end of each episode.
Well here I am - feels like the end... but I've learned nothing
except maybe... sandwiches from New Jersey really *are*
worth the trip?

JIMMY

Told ya! Jersey Sandwiches *rule*!!

FRANKIE
(pointing to Jimmy to prove her point)
Exactly! Jimmy's right!

JIMMY

I am?

FRANKIE

Because maybe the point of everything is just to laugh and
have as much fun as you can while you can... and that
includes stopping to get delicious sandwiches once in
awhile. The meaning of life... is *life*. You get one shot. So,
why not live the heck out of it?

KID

...Huh.

FRANKIE

'Cause it's not about the *one* lesson learned at the end of
each episode. It's about the *same* lesson in *every* great story...
Be There For Each Other. Whether it's your actual family or
your chosen family. It's not 'me, me, me.' It's 'we, we, we.'
And yes I know that sounds like This Little Piggy Went to
Market... but that's actually the super secret message of that
nursery rhyme. Some people think it's about pigs being sent

FRANKIE (cont)

to the butcher for slaughter, right? Fattening some up, while others aren't ready for sale so they stay back at the farm. But I think it's actually about how certain people choose to live - and how the seven deadly sins can easily take hold. One piggy went shopping at the market: greed and pride. One piggy stayed home: lazy sloth. One had roast beef: glutton. One had none: envious and wrathful. But the last piggy. The last one said, no... we should't give in to our basest nature. And then that piggy said 'we, we, we' all the way _home_. *(strums guitar and lightly sings)* We, we, _WE_... gotta stick together. *(talking again)* Otherwise we get slaughtered.

KID

...What about lust?

FRANKIE

I didn't say it was a perfect metaphor!!

The Kid nods. Frankie smiles.

KNOCK-KNOCK-KNOCK from the front door.

MELISSA

I'll get it.

She scampers to the front door and opens it. It's Norman Lear. He tips his hat hello.

NORMAN LEAR

Hey there, everyone!

MELISSA, JIMMY & FRANKIE

NORM!

                              KID
...Norman Lear. ...What are you doing here?

                         NORMAN LEAR
Time to go, kid.

                              KID
Go, like... home?

                         NORMAN LEAR
We, we, we.... All the way home.

                            FRANKIE
I knew it! It _IS_ the perfect metaphor.

                    *Frankie plays one awesome chord on the guitar
                    then raises her hand in victory!*

                              KID
...Yeah, I still don't get it.

                    *Frankie is about to try explaining again when
                    Norman Lear raises his hand slightly.*

                         NORMAN LEAR
Frankie, dear - if I may?

                            FRANKIE
Would you like the guitar?

                         NORMAN LEAR
...I'm good.

                    *Frankie gestures grandly, giving Norman Lear
                    the floor.*

NORMAN LEAR

It's like this, Kid. Life isn't about what YOU do. It's what WE do. Together. It's about the people you meet, the relationships you make, and sticking together. It's why I love being a writer. We get to build communities out of thin air! From a completely blank page we can dream up an entire world and create characters like these *(gestures to the Friends)* -- then before ya know it, hundreds of _actual_ people are working together to make that dream a reality. Actors, directors, producers, set and costume designers, makeup artists, lights camera action! From one tiny spark of an idea, comes a team of folks to make it happen. Then it goes out into the world where it can make _millions_ of people feel better about life -- even if only for a little while. And to _me_...? That's the greatest gift there is. But if you have that ability to MAKE comedy... and DON'T...? Then that's a _tragedy_. For all of us.

KID

...Okay. I get it now.

NORMAN LEAR

Good! Cuz it's time to vamoose!

The Kid looks around.

KID

Wow, so I guess... this is goodbye?

Frankie, Melissa, and Jimmy are standing together. They nod and wave, maybe a bit emotional. After a beat, Jimmy runs over and HUGS the Kid. Then Melissa and Frankie run over for a big GROUP HUG.

41

NORMAN LEAR
All right, all right - enough sappy stuff. Gotta get this kid back home.

>*They break the hug. The Kid walks to Norman and is right by the door.*

MELISSA
Wait! You forgot something.

>*Melissa brings the laptop to the Kid.*

MELISSA
All fixed.

KID
Oh, cool. Yeah -- probably gonna need this.

JIMMY
Wait! Uh... I got something for ya, too...

>*Not wanting to be left out, Jimmy looks around for something to give the Kid. He looks at his sandwich, nah can't give that away. Instead he grabs a fortune cookie from the to-go bag and runs to the Kid.*

JIMMY
Fortune Cookie! Case ya get hungry on the way.

>*The Kid nods.*

KID
Thanks.... *(looks at the rest of the friends)*. For everything.

Kid turns to Norman.

                    KID
So how do we do this?

                NORMAN LEAR
Everything you need... is in your hands.

                    KID
                ("gets it")
Oh! Like the answer I need has been inside me this whole
time?

                NORMAN LEAR
No, I mean the remote. In your hand. Just hit the little
"HOME" button.

                    KID
The "home" button... that's it?

                NORMAN LEAR
Easy-peasey-lemon-squeezey.

                    KID
Why didn't I think of that?

            Kid lifts the remote... squints, bracing for
            impact... And presses the Home button.

            Norman gives an EAR TUG to the PROMPTS
            off-stage who then enter as the lights go funky
            and weird while the Prompts do the "Wayne's
            World" flashback move again: wiggling their
            arms in front of their faces as they say:

THE 3 PROMPTS
(wiggling arms in front of faces)
Doo-doo-loo-doo. Doo-doo-loo-doo. Doo-doo-loo-doo.
Doo-doo-loo-doo.

The lights go black.

SCENE 8

> *After a beat, the lights come up on the Kid
> standing in the middle of the room holding the
> remote, laptop and fortune cookie. The kid looks
> around, touches their body: am I real? Am I
> really here?*

KID

Oh my gosh, it's over - I'm back!

> *The Kid looks at the fortune cookie.*

KID

...Huh.

> *The Kid opens the fortune cookie and reads the
> slip of paper inside.*

KID

"You Will Find Your True Passion."

> *The Kid smiles, nods... then an idea strikes!*

KID

Wait a minute! The glimpse wasn't just telling me to find my passion... it was teaching me everything I need to know about writing -- and life!

> *As the Kid talks, lights rise on the characters we've seen so far -- and stay up until noted. (Or they can just enter for a beat then exit.)*
>
> *LIGHTS UP ON: Melissa, Jimmy and Frankie.*

KID

Embrace big ensembles. The more the merrier!

> *LIGHTS UP ON: Jacques, Kathleen and Chase doing spit takes.*

KID

Sometimes physical comedy produces the purest laugh.

> *LIGHTS UP ON: Sylvia, Ruth and Blair.*

KID

Listen to your elders. They've seen a thing or two -- and can also be hilarious.

> *LIGHTS UP ON: Some of the Catchphrases.*

KID

Louder, faster, funnier is always good advice.

> *LIGHTS UP ON: Norman Lear.*

KID

...Do something meaningful with your life. Before you regret the road not traveled.

The Kid races to a chair/sofa to sit as they open the laptop and begin typing.

KID
(as they type)
Fade in. Interior. New York City Apartment. Day.

The Kid smiles then continues typing as the lights fade on everyone.

SCENE 9

From the dark we hear:

GRAN (IN THE DARK)
Hey, Kid.... Kid, wake up. It's time for school.

Lights up. Gran sits nearby gently waking up the Kid who fell asleep while writing. The laptop is closed on the Kid's lap.

KID
(sleepy)
What? What time is it?

GRAN
Time to get going. You don't wanna be late.

KID
Okay. Wow! I had the weirdest dream.

GRAN

Oh yeah? What was it about?

KID

...I... can't remember exactly? I just know it was weird. And maybe life-changing?

GRAN

You're right. That's weird.

KID

Anyway, I, uh. I'm gonna work on those college applications this week because... I think I _do_ wanna be a writer.

GRAN
(quietly pleased)

...Okay.

KID

And maybe... try writing sitcoms? Or at least comedy.

GRAN

So - no dark, brooding dramas?

KID

The world's dark enough, right.

GRAN

Might as well make 'em laugh.

KID

Exactly. So, uh... here.

The Kid opens the laptop and shows it to Gran.

GRAN

What's this?

KID

I stayed up all night writing it.

> *Gran reads for a beat then LAUGHS loud and hearty. Gran looks at the Kid.*

GRAN

...You found your true passion.

> *Gran pats the Kid on the knee then stands up.*

KID

Aren't ya gonna read the rest of it?

GRAN

Of course.

> *KNOCK-KNOCK-KNOCK on the front door.*

GRAN

Except not right now. That's my Bingo date.
(heading off to bedroom)
Grab the door, will ya? I gotta get my stuff.

> *Gran stops by the bedroom door.*

GRAN

Hey, Kid. ...Ya did good.

> *Gran smiles then exits.*

> *The Kid smiles back, takes a moment to feel*

proud, then goes to the front door and opens it.

Standing at the door is Norman Lear, wearing his usual jaunty hat.

NORMAN LEAR
Hey there, Kid. What's happening?

KID
(with a big smile)

Norm!!

END OF PLAY.